Lotus Pond by Moonlight

And Other Selected Prose by Zhu Ziqing

Second improved edition

Translated by Haiying Zhang

Translation and cover photograph copyright
© Haiying Zhang 2006

ISBN: 978-0-9551672-0-1

www.haiying.org.uk

First published and printed in the United Kingdom in 2006

Reprinted in 2007

Acknowledgement

Thanks for all the support I received in translating this book.

Special thanks to Susanna Gladwin, creative writing tutor at Middlesex University; Anna Webber, language tutor at Waltham Forest College and my blind friend George Foremann. They offered valuable comments and suggestions and helped make this book "sparkle".

CONTENTS

Introduction

Zhu Ziqing (朱自清) was an outstanding Chinese prose writer, poet and educator. He was born in Zhejiang Province in 1898.

Zhu Ziqing wrote both poetry and prose, but he is better known as an essay-writer than a poet. He was educated at Beijing University. After qualifying in 1925, he took a position as professor of Chinese literature at Qinghua University.

In 1931-1932 he studied English literature and linguistics in London, and travelled to five countries in Europe. He returned to China in July 1932, and became the dean of the Chinese Language Department at Qinghua University.

He started writing poetry early in his career and is best known for his long poem "Huimie" [Destruction] (1923). His collections of prose include "Beiying" [The View of My Father's Back] (1928) and "Ni wo" [You and Me] (1936).

Upright, diligent and a tireless teacher, Zhu Ziqing was regarded as a model modern scholar by his students and colleagues. Two of his most respected pieces of prose *The View of My Father's Back* and *Lotus Pond by Moonlight* are included in this book.

Zhu died in August 1948. In August 1978, three decades after his death, "Ziqing Pavilion" was built at Qinghua University in his memory. In April 1987, during the anniversary of the founding of the university, a white-marble statue of Zhu was erected on the bank of the lotus pond.

In this collection, the translator selected five of Zhu's most famous prose pieces and translated them into English. One piece is about a person *The View of My Father's Back*, another describes the passing of time *Swiftly*, and the other three are about nature and scenery. Zhu is famous for his descriptions of nature and scenery. He has the ability to make people believe that they are there seeing and feeling what he is experiencing. It is as if when reading his work you can touch the trees, feel the mist, taste the water, and smell the grass...

The five pieces of prose were all written in the 1920's. *Lotus Pond by Moonlight* is one of Zhu Ziqing's masterpieces (1927). It was written after the coup of 12 April in 1927 [the 4.12 Coup]. The author was left depressed by the confusion and disorder caused by the Coup. He became down hearted so he said directly at the beginning of the piece "I have been feeling uneasy these days." He felt no sense of freedom in daytime, so he found freedom of expression with nature at night. Even though his night-time escape to nature was short, it refreshed him. He came to the lotus pond and found peace there in the vast moonlit night with the fragrance of lotus blossoms. While reading this work the reader should remember the turmoil and the restrictions he was under as a writer in time of political unrest. It may be necessary for today's reader to read between the lines to get the full meaning of this piece of work.

The aim of this book is to give people outside China a chance to become better acquainted with Chinese poetry and prose, while offering Chinese readers a chance to see the work in English translation.

Haiying Zhang
Westcliff-on-sea, 2006

匆匆

燕子去了，有再来的时候；杨柳枯了，有再青的时候；桃花谢了，有再开的时候。但是，聪明的，你告诉我，我们的日子为什么一去不复返呢？——是有人偷了他们罢：那是谁？又藏在何处呢？是他们自己逃走了罢：现在又到了哪里呢？

我不知道他们给了我多少日子；但我的手确乎是渐渐空虚了。在默默里算着，八千多日子已经从我手中溜去；像针尖上一滴水滴在大海里，我的日子滴在时间的流里，没有声音，也没有影子。我不禁头涔涔而泪潸潸了。

去的尽管去了，来的尽管来着；去来的中间，又怎样地匆匆呢？早上我起来的时候，小屋里射进两三方斜斜的太阳。太阳他有脚啊，轻轻悄悄地挪移了；我也茫茫然跟着旋转。于是——洗手的时候，日子从水盆里过去；吃饭的时候，日子从饭碗里过去；默默时，便从凝然的双眼前过去。我觉察他去的匆匆了，伸出手遮挽时，他又从遮挽着的手边过去，天黑时，我躺在床上，他便伶伶俐俐地从我身上跨过，从我脚边飞去了。等我睁开眼和太阳再见，这算又溜走了一日。我掩着面叹息。但是新来的日子的影儿又开始在叹息里闪过了。

Swiftly

Swallows depart, they will come back again; willows wither, they will be green again; peach flowers fade, they will bloom again. But clever as you are, please tell me, why do our days pass never come back again? Has someone stolen them? But who could that be? And where have they been hidden? Have they run away by themselves? Where are they now?

I don't know how many days I have been given, but I do know that something is slipping from my grasp little by little. I'm counting in silence: over eight thousand days have slipped through my fingers, like a drop of water from the point of a needle into the sea. My days are dripping into the river of time, no sound, no shape. I find sweat on my forehead and tears in my eyes!

Time gone never returns; time coming is still to come. Between time coming and time going, how hastily time goes! When I get up in the morning, two or three squares of sunshine lean into my small room. Oh, the sun, it has feet. It is moving silently and slightly, but I'm rolling with it at a loss. When I'm washing my hands, my days are flying away from my basin; when I'm having my meal, my days are passing across my bowl; when I'm lost in thought, my days are departing from in front of my gazing eyes. When I notice that they're going too quickly and want to pull them back with my hands, they flee away from my hands. When it's dark I lie on my bed, they stride across me swiftly and fly away from my feet. When I open my eyes to see the sun, another day has passed! With my hands on my face, the shadows of the new day flash away with my sighs.

在逃去如飞的日子里，在千门万户的世界里的我能做些什么呢？只有徘徊罢了，只有匆匆罢了；在八千多日的匆匆里，除徘徊外，又剩些什么呢？过去的日子如轻烟，被微风吹散了，如薄雾，被初阳蒸融了；我留着些什么痕迹呢？我何曾留着像游丝样的痕迹呢？我赤裸裸来到这世界，转眼间也将赤裸裸的回去罢？但不能平的，为什么偏要白白走这一遭啊？

你聪明的，告诉我，我们的日子为什么一去不复返呢？

（写于 1922 年 3 月）

In days fleeing and flying, what can I do in this crowded world? Only wander while time hurries by. In those eight thousand days swiftly passed gone forever, what else have I left except wandering aimlessly? Days passed like light smoke, scattered by the gentle wind; like mist, melted by the morning sun. What marks have I made? Have I left any traces like gossamer at all? I came to this world with nothing and will go away without anything. But what's unfair is why I should have come to this world in vain!

Clever as you are, please tell me, why do our days go never to return?

- Written in March 1922

春

盼望着，盼望着，东风来了，春天的脚步近了。

一切都像刚睡醒的样子，欣欣然张开了眼。山朗润起来了，水长起来了，太阳的脸红起来了。

小草偷偷地从土里钻出来，嫩嫩的，绿绿的。园子里，田野里，瞧去，一大片一大片满是的。坐着，躺着，打两个滚，踢几脚球，赛几趟跑，捉几回迷藏。风轻悄悄的，草绵软软的。 桃树、杏树、梨树，你不让我，我不让你，都开满了花赶趟儿。红的像火，粉的像霞， 白的像雪。花里带着甜味，闭了眼，树上仿佛已经满是桃儿、杏儿、梨儿！花下成千成百的 蜜蜂嗡嗡地闹着，大小的蝴蝶飞来飞去。野花遍地是：杂样儿，有名字的，没名字的，散在草丛里，像眼睛，像星星，还眨呀眨的。

"吹面不寒杨柳风"，不错的，像母亲的手抚摸着你。风里带来些新翻的泥土的气息， 混着青草味，还有各种花的香，都在微微润湿的空气里酝酿。鸟儿将窠巢安在繁花嫩叶当中，高兴起来了，呼朋引伴地卖弄清脆的喉咙，唱出宛转的曲子，与轻风流水应和着。牛背上牧童的短笛，这时候也成天在嘹亮地响。

Spring

Hoping, hoping, the wind from the east is coming; spring is gently drawing near.

The world slowly awakes from its winter sleep, eyes opening to spring's new beginning. The mountains are wearing their coats of spring greenery; water is rising; the face of the sun is reddening.

Grass is peeking out of the earth shyly, so tender, so green. In the garden, in the field, wherever you look, your eyes are filled with big patches of green! People are sitting or lying, rolling on the grass, playing football, having a race, playing hide-and-seek... The wind is so gentle; the grass is so soft. Peach trees, apricot trees, pear trees, you are boasting, I am boasting, all in blossom in a hurry, red as a blazing fire, pink as the evening sun, white as the winter snow. Sweetness is in those flowers. If you close your eyes, as if trees were full of peaches, apricots and pears! Thousands of bees are buzzing under the flowers, big and small butterflies are flying here and there. All kinds of wild flowers are everywhere, some with names some without, all beautifully scattered in the grass like eyes, like stars, twinkling, twinkling...

"The wind through the willows is not cold" Ah yes, like your mother's fingers gently caressing you. The wind carries the smell of just turned earth, mixed with the perfumes of grass and wild flowers, fermenting in the moist warm air. Birds are making their nests in full-blown flowers and feeble leaves, so joyful are they now, showing off their clear and sharp voices, singing sweet songs, together with the light wind and the flowing river. Cowherds are playing their bamboo flutes on the backs of cows all day, loudly.

雨是最寻常的，一下就是三两天。可别恼，看，像牛毛，像花针，像细丝，密密地斜织着，人家屋顶上全笼着一层薄烟。树叶子却绿得发亮，小草也青得逼你的眼。傍晚时候，上灯了，一点点黄晕的光，烘托出一片安静而和平的夜。乡下去，小路上，石桥边，撑起伞慢慢走着的人；还有地里工作的农夫，披着蓑，戴着笠的。他们的草屋，稀稀疏疏的在雨里静默着。

天上风筝渐渐多了，地上孩子也多了。城里乡下，家家户户，老老小小，他们也赶趟儿似的，一个个都出来了。舒活舒活筋骨，抖擞抖擞精神，各做各的一份事去。

"一年之计在于春" 刚起头儿，有的是工夫，有的是希望。春天像刚落地的娃娃，从头到脚都是新的，它生长着。春天像小姑娘，花枝招展的，笑着，走着。春天像健壮的青年，有铁一般的胳膊和腰脚，领着我们上前去。

（写于 1925 年 10 月）

Rain is the usual thing, two or three days without stopping. But be patient, look, it looks like cow fur, like needles, like thin threads... closely woven, leaning forward to the ground. The roofs of houses are shrouded in light smoke. But the leaves are so green, they are shining; the grass is so green, it is entering into your eyes. In the evening, lights are on. Little lights are here and there with yellow crowns, setting off a silent and peaceful night. In the countryside, on the pathway, by the stone bridge, some people with their umbrellas are walking slowly. Peasants in the fields wear raincoats of straw on their backs and straw hats on their heads. Their straw houses stand in the rain silently, thinly scattered.

More and more kites are appearing in the sky, more and more children are appearing on the ground as well. In cities and in the countryside, all the families, old and young people, all in a hurry, are coming out of their houses, stretching their arms and legs... full of energy, high spirited, all doing their own thing.

"The year starts with spring", it's a beginning, full of time, full of hope. Spring is like a newborn baby, fresh from head to foot, it is growing. Spring is like a girl, charming and glamorous, she is smiling; she is walking. Spring is like a young man whose arms and waist and feet are as strong as steel, he is leading us forward.

- Written in October 1925

荷塘月色

这几天心里颇不宁静。今晚在院子里坐着乘凉，忽然想起日日走过的荷塘，在这满月的光里，总该另有一番样子吧。月亮渐渐地升高了，墙外马路上孩子们的欢笑，已经听不见了；妻在屋里拍着闰儿，迷迷糊糊地哼着眠歌。我悄悄地披了大衫，带上门出去。

沿着荷塘，是一条曲折的小煤屑路。这是一条幽僻的路；白天也少人走，夜晚更加寂寞。荷塘四面，长着许多树，蓊蓊郁郁的。路的一旁，是些杨柳，和一些不知道名字的树。没有月光的晚上，这路上阴森森的，有些怕人。今晚却很好，虽然月光也还是淡淡的。

路上只我一个人，背着手踱着。这一片天地好像是我的；我也像超出了平常的自己，到了另一世界里。我爱热闹，也爱冷静；爱群居，也爱独处。像今晚上，一个人在这苍茫的月下，什么都可以想，什么都可以不想，便觉是个自由的人。白天里一定要做的事，一定要说的话，现在都可不理。这是独处的妙处，我且受用这无边的荷香月色好了。

曲曲折折的荷塘上面，弥望的是田田的叶子。叶子出水很高，像亭亭的舞女的裙。层层的叶子中间，零星地点缀着些白花，有袅娜地开着的，有羞涩地打着朵儿的；正如一粒粒的明珠，又如碧天

Lotus Pond by Moonlight

I have been feeling uneasy these days. Sitting in the cool of the evening in my yard, I suddenly think of the lotus pond, which I pass by everyday. In this full moonlight, might it look different? The moon is higher; gone is the laughter of children by the road outside the wall. My wife is stroking our son, Run-er, drowsily humming a lullaby. Quietly, I put on my coat, close the door and go out.

Beside the lotus pond there is a small tortuous cinder path. This is a secluded road even by day, more isolated still at night. Around the pond, there are many trees rich in leaves, lush and green. There are some willows along the path, and some trees whose names I do not know. When there is no moonlight the road and pond have a haunted disconcerting feel to them. Tonight is not bad, even though the moon looks pale.

Only I am on the road, walking with my hands behind my back as if everything here belongs to me, and it seems that I am no longer myself and have come into another world, a changed reality. I like being in crowd or being in silence, living with others or being alone. Tonight for instance, I am in this boundless moonlight by myself. I can think of anything or nothing, conscious of being a free man. Things that must be done or words that must be said during the day cannot bother me now. This is the beauty of being alone. Let me just benefit from this vast moonlit night with the lotuses.

Above the winding lotus pond, leaves with quartered lines fill my eyes. Leaves are high above the water, like the skirts of slim dancing girls. In those layers of leaves, dotted with white flowers here and there, some are gracefully in bloom, some shyly in bud,

里的星星，又如刚出浴的美人。微风过处，送来缕缕清香，仿佛远处高楼上渺茫的歌声似的。这时候叶子与花也有一丝的颤动，像闪电般，霎时传过荷塘的那边去了。叶子本是肩并肩密密地挨着，这便宛然有了一道凝碧的波痕。叶子底下是脉脉的流水，遮住了，不能见一些颜色；而叶子却更见风致了。

月光如流水一般，静静地泻在这一片叶子和花上。薄薄的青雾浮起在荷塘里。叶子和花仿佛在牛乳中洗过一样；又像笼着轻纱的梦。虽然是满月，天上却有一层淡淡的云，所以不能朗照；但我以为这恰是到了好处——酣眠固不可少，小睡也别有风味的。月光是隔了树照过来的，高处丛生的灌木，落下参差的斑驳的黑影，峭楞楞如鬼一般；弯弯的杨柳的稀疏的倩影，却又像是画在荷叶上。塘中的月色并不均匀；但光与影有着和谐的旋律，如梵婀玲上奏着的名曲。

荷塘的四面，远远近近，高高低低都是树，而杨柳最多。这些树将一片荷塘重重围住；只在小路一旁，漏着几段空隙，像是特为月光留下的。树色一例是阴阴的，乍看像一团烟雾；但杨柳的丰姿，便在烟雾里也辨得出。树梢上隐隐约约的是一带远山，只有些大意罢了。树缝里也漏着一两点路灯光，没精打采的，是渴睡人的眼。这时候最热闹的，要数树上的蝉声与水里的蛙声；但热闹是它们的，我什么也没有。

like scattered pearls, like stars in the clear sky, like beautiful girls just after a bath. Where gentle wind passes, there are wisps of light perfume, like faint songs coming from distant high buildings. At this moment, there is a tiny thrill between the flowers and leaves, like lightning, streaking across the lotus pond suddenly. Leaves are shoulder to shoulder, closely standing together, now there is a patch of green water. Water is flowing silently under the leaves, it is hidden, no colour can be seen, but more charming are the leaves.

Moonlight is like flowing water, pouring peacefully onto the leaves and flowers. Filmy mists rise in the lotus pond. The leaves and flowers are as if washed in cow's milk, like a dream covered with light yarn. Although it is a full moon, there is a thin layer of cloud in the sky. The moon cannot get through to give full light. But I think it's just about perfect - although sound sleeps are necessary, naps also have a special flavour. Moonlight is passing through trees. Bushes from higher ground cast irregular black shadows, like ghosts. The beautiful shadows of bending willows are sparsely drawn on the lotus leaves. Moonlight in the pond is not even, but lightness and shadows are in harmony, like sublime music played on a violin.

The area around the lotus pond for a great distance in all directions is thickly wooded with willows. Only by the path are some gaps, as if left on purpose only for the moonlight. All the trees look dark, like smoky mist at first glance, but the beautiful look of willows can be recognised even in fog and smoke. On the treetops there are only some indistinct images of unclear mountains in the distance. Between the cracks of leaves leak out one or two streetlights, dull and gloomy, like the eyes of a sleepy person. At this time, the noisiest things are cicadas in the trees and frogs in the water, but the excitement is theirs, not mine.

忽然想起采莲的事情来了。采莲是江南的旧俗，似乎很早就有，而六朝时为盛；从诗歌里可以约略知道。采莲的是少年的女子，她们是荡着小船，唱着艳歌去的。采莲人不用说很多，还有看采莲的人。那是一个热闹的季节，也是一个风流的季节。梁元帝《采莲赋》里说得好：

于是妖童媛女，荡舟心许；鷁首徐回，兼传羽杯；櫂将移而藻挂，船欲动而萍开。尔其纤腰束素，迁延顾步；夏始春余，叶嫩花初，恐沾裳而浅笑，畏倾船而敛裾。

可见当时嬉游的光景了。这真是有趣的事，可惜我们现在早已无福消受了。

于是又记起《西洲曲》里的句子：

采莲南塘秋，莲花过人头；低头弄莲子，莲子清如水。今晚若有采莲人，这儿的莲花也算得"过人头"了；只不见一些流水的影子，是不行的。这令我到底惦着江南了。——这样想着，猛一抬头，不觉已是自己的门前；轻轻地推门进去，什么声息也没有，妻已睡熟好久了。

（写于 1927 年 7 月）

Suddenly the matter of picking lotuses occurred to me. It is an ancient custom in southern China, but most fashionable in the period of the Six Dynasties. This can be known a little through poetry. Young ladies used to pick lotuses, singing love songs as their boats swayed in the ripples of rivers. It goes without saying that just as there were many people picking lotuses, there were many people watching as well. That was a busy time, but also a time full of love affairs. In a poem *Picking Lotuses* by Yuan Emperor in the Liang Dynasty, says:

"So, enchanting children and charming girls are in swinging boats with love in their hearts; looking back now and again, passing cups of feathers. They move the paddles, and the paddles are hung with water grass. When the boats are about to move, the lotuses open. Their slim waists girdled with plain silk. They are lingering and loitering... Late spring, beginning of summer; leaves are gentle and flowers are new. Afraid of being splashed, they are in gentle smiles. Afraid of falling into water, they pull back their skirts."

From this, you can get a picture of leisure time in that era. It is really interesting, but we do not have such good luck now.

I also remember the lines in the *West Water Song*:

"In the south pond in autumn, picking lotuses, / Lotus flowers are higher than our heads. / Bend down to play with lotus seeds, / They are as clear as water, it seems." If there were people picking lotuses tonight, the flowers could also be said to be 'higher than heads', but it is no good without seeing the shadows of the flowing water. This makes me miss the South. Walking lost in thought, looking up suddenly, I am already in front of my own house, pushing the door quietly, not a sound inside; my wife has been in a deep sleep for quite a while.

- Written in July 1927

背影

我与父亲不相见已二年余了，我最不能忘记的是他的背影。那年冬天，祖母死了，父亲的差使也交卸了，正是祸不单行的日子，我从北京到徐州，打算跟着父亲奔丧回家。到徐州见着父亲，看见满院狼藉的东西，又想起祖母，不禁簌簌地流下眼泪。父亲说，"事已如此，不必难过，好在天无绝人之路！"

回家变卖典质，父亲还了亏空；又借钱办了丧事。这些日子，家中光景很是惨淡，一半为了丧事，一半为了父亲赋闲。丧事完毕，父亲要到南京谋事，我也要回北京念书，我们便同行。

到南京时，有朋友约去游逛，勾留了一日；第二日上午便须渡江到浦口，下午上车北去。父亲因为事忙，本已说定不送我，叫旅馆里一个熟识的茶房陪我同去。他再三嘱咐茶房，甚是仔细。但他终于不放心，怕茶房不妥帖；颇踌躇了一会。其实我那年已二十岁，北京已来往过两三次，是没有甚么要紧的了。他踌躇了一会，终于决定还是自己送我。我两三回劝他不必去；他只说，"不要紧，他们去不好！"

我们过了江，进了车站。我买票，他忙着照看行李。行李太多

The View of My Father's Back

I haven't seen my father for over two years but the thing that stays in my mind is the view of his back. In the winter that my grandmother died, my father lost his job. That was the time when misfortunes never came singly. I went to Xuzhou from Beijing, going to make some funeral arrangements with my father. I saw him in Xuzhou. The yard was in a mess. Thinking of my grandmother, I couldn't hold my tears back. My father said, "Things have happened, don't worry, we will find a way."

He pawned something, paid his debts, and borrowed some money for the funeral. In those days our house was full of gloom, what with the funeral and father being out of work. After the funeral, my father was going to find a job in Nanjing, and I was going to study in Beijing, so we went together.

I stayed in Nanjing for one day, because my friends invited me to look around. The next day, I had to take a ship to Pukou in the morning and a train to the north in the afternoon. As he was very busy, my father said he was not going to see me off and asked a friend in the teahouse of a hotel to accompany me. He told the friend again and again what to do, carefully. In the end, he still didn't feel at ease, couldn't count on the friend and hesitated for a while. In fact, I was twenty years old already, and had been to Beijing two or three times, there was no need for him to worry about me. He hesitated for a while, and decided to see me off himself in the end. I tried two or three times to persuade him not to go, but he simply replied, "Never mind, they cannot be trusted to get it right."

We crossed the river, entered the train station. I bought a ticket and he was busy looking after the baggage. Too much of it,

了，得向脚夫行些小费，才可过去。他便又忙着和他们讲价钱。我那时真是聪明过分，总觉他说话不大漂亮，非自己插嘴不可。但他终于讲定了价钱；就送我上车。他给我拣定了靠车门的一张椅子；我将他给我做的紫毛大衣铺好坐位。他嘱我路上小心，夜里警醒些，不要受凉。又嘱托茶房好好照应我。我心里暗笑他的迂；他们只认得钱，托他们直是白托！而且我这样大年纪的人，难道还不能料理自己么？唉，我现在想想，那时真是太聪明了！

我说道，"爸爸，你走吧。"他望车外看了看，说，"我买几个橘子去。你就在此地，不要走动。"我看那边月台的栅栏外有几个卖东西的等着顾客。走到那边月台，须穿过铁道，须跳下去又爬上去。父亲是一个胖子，走过去自然要费事些。我本来要去的，他不肯，只好让他去。我看见他戴着黑布小帽，穿着黑布大马褂，深青布棉袍，蹒跚地走到铁道边，慢慢探身下去，尚不大难。可是他穿过铁道，要爬上那边月台，就不容易了。他用两手攀着上面，两脚再向上缩；他肥胖的身子向左微倾，显出努力的样子。这时我看见他的背影，我的泪很快地流下来了。我赶紧拭干了泪，怕他看见，也怕别人看见。我再向外看时，他已抱了朱红的橘子望回走了。过铁道时，他先将橘子散放在地上，自己慢慢爬下，再抱起橘子走。

we had to pay some tips to get it through, so he was busy bargaining with a porter. I was too clever then, feeling that he couldn't get it right without me. Finally, he fixed the price and saw me off on the train. He picked a seat for me near the door, and I put the coat with purple fur that he made on the seat. He told me to be careful during the journey, be alert at night, not to catch a cold. Once again he asked a man in the teahouse to look after me. I smiled to myself at his over-anxiousness. They were only after the money. There was no use asking them at all. What's more, a person of my age, couldn't he look after himself? Ah, when I think of it now, I was too clever at that time.

I said, "Papa, you may go now." He looked out of the train, and said, "I'm going to buy you some oranges, you stay here, don't move." I saw some people selling things and waiting for customers beyond the platform. To walk across, he had to jump off this platform, go across the rails and climb up that platform. My father was fat, so it would take him some effort to get there. I wanted to go, but he wouldn't let me go, so he went there instead of me. I saw him wearing a black cloth hat, in a big black robe and a black cotton gown. He walked to the edge of the railway haltingly. It was not too difficult for him to bend his body down from the platform on this side, but it was not easy for him to cross the railway tracks and climb up the platform on the other side. His hands held the edge of the platform, his feet were stretching upwards. His fat body was leaning slightly to the left. It seemed that he was straining from the effort. When I saw his back view, tears started at once to fall. I hurriedly wiped them away in order to avoid being seen by him and the other people. When I looked out again, he was walking back, holding the oranges in his arms. When he was going to cross the rails, he put the oranges on the ground first, slowly climbed down, then walked back, holding the

到这边时，我赶紧去搀他。他和我走到车上，将橘子一股脑儿放在我的皮大衣上。于是扑扑衣上的泥土，心里很轻松似的，过一会说，"我走了；到那边来信！"我望着他走出去。他走了几步，回过头看见我，说，"进去吧，里边没人。"等他的背影混入来来往往的人里，再找不着了，我便进来坐下，我的眼泪又来了。

近几年来，父亲和我都是东奔西走，家中光景是一日不如一日。他少年出外谋生，独力支持，做了许多大事。那知老境却如此颓唐！他触目伤怀，自然情不能自已。情郁于中，自然要发之于外；家庭琐屑便往往触他之怒。他待我渐渐不同往日。但最近两年的不见，他终于忘却我的不好，只是惦记着我，惦记着我的儿子。我北来后，他写了一信给我，信中说道，"我身体平安，惟膀子疼痛利害，举箸提笔，诸多不便，大约大去之期不远矣。"我读到此处，在晶莹的泪光中，又看见那肥胖的，青布棉袍，黑布马褂的背影。唉！我不知何时再能与他相见！

（写于 1925 年 10 月）

oranges in his arms again. When he was on this side, I went up to support him immediately. We entered the train. He put all the oranges on my leather coat and brushed the dust and mud off his clothes. He seemed delighted. After a little while, he said, "I'm going now, write to me when you get there." I followed him and saw him walk out. After a few paces, he looked back, and said, "Get in, no one is there." When his back disappeared in the crowd, I couldn't find him again, I got in and sat down, my tears came back again.

During these years, my father and I were busy going here and there. The situation at home was getting worse and worse. He made his living when he was very young, did a lot of great things by himself. He never realized that he would be so dejected when he got older. He felt sick at heart, feeling depressed when confronted by minor family problems. Anyway, it seemed to me that his attitude towards me had changed. After two years being separated he at last forgot my faults and only showed his longings for my son and I. When I got to Beijing he wrote me a letter. It said, "I am well except that my shoulders ache a lot; holding chopsticks or a pen, causes too much inconvenience; it seems that I will die soon." When I read this, through my clear tears, the view of his fat back came to me again - in his black robe and cotton gown. Ah, when will I see him again?

- Written in October 1925

桨声灯影里的秦怀河

一九二三年八月的一晚，我和平伯同游秦淮河；平伯是初泛，我是重来了。我们雇了一只"七板子"，在夕阳已去，皎月方来的时候，便下了船。于是桨声汩汩，我们开始领略那晃荡着蔷薇色的历史的秦淮河的滋味了。

秦淮河里的船，比北京万甡园，颐和园的船好，比西湖的船好，比扬州瘦西湖的船也好。这几处的船不是觉着笨，就是觉着简陋、局促；都不能引起乘客们的情韵，如秦淮河的船一样。秦淮河的船约略可分为两种：一是大船；一是小船，就是所谓"七板子"。大船舱口阔大，可容二三十人。里面陈设着字画和光洁的红木家具，桌上一律嵌着冰凉的大理石面。窗格雕镂颇细，使人起柔腻之感。窗格里映着红色蓝色的玻璃；玻璃上有精致的花纹，也颇悦人目。"七板子"规模虽不及大船，但那淡蓝色的栏干，空敞的舱，也足系人情思。而最出色处却在它的舱前。舱前是甲板上的一部。上面有弧形的顶，两边用疏疏的栏干支着。里面通常放着两张藤的躺椅。

Qin Huai River in Sound Of Oars
And Light Reflections

On an August night in 1923, Ping Bo and I visited the Qinhuai River together. It was the first time for Ping Bo but the second time for me. We hired a "Seven Paddle Boards". When the evening sun had gone, the bright moon rose. We got on the boat. The sound of oars was bubbling. We began to enjoy the flavour of the Qinhuai River rippling with the history of pink love affairs.

Boats on the Qinhuai River are better than boats in Beijing's Wang Sheng Garden, better than the boats at the Summer Palace, better than the boats on the West Lake, better even than the boats on the slim Yang Zhou West Lake. If it is not because the boats in those places are clumsy, then it is because they are too simple or too narrow. They don't have the lingering charm that the Qinhuai River boats do. Roughly, there are two types of boats on the Qinhuai River: one is a big boat, the other is a small boat called the "Seven Paddle Boards". The entrance of a big boat is wide and it is big enough to hold twenty or thirty people. A big boat is furnished with calligraphic paintings and red wood furniture, smooth and shining; the table surfaces are of icy marble. Finely carved window squares make people feel soft and tender, red or blue windowpanes with exquisite designs shine inside, quite pleasing to the eye. Although a "Seven Paddle Boards" is not as large as a big one, the light blue balustrades and the spacious cabin are beautiful enough to acquire people's affection. The best place is in its bow, which forms a part of its deck. There is an arched ceiling on the top, supported by widely spaced columns on both sides. Normally, there are two deck chairs made of rattan.

躺下，可以谈天，可以望远，可以顾盼两岸的河房。大船上也有这个，便在小船上更觉清隽罢了。舱前的顶下，一律悬着灯彩；灯的多少，明暗，彩苏的精粗，艳晦，是不一的。但好歹总还你一个灯彩。这灯彩实在是最能钩人的东西。夜幕垂垂地下来时，大小船上都点起灯火。从两重玻璃里映出那辐射着的黄黄的散光，反晕出一片朦胧的烟霭；透过这烟霭，在黯黯的水波里，又逗起缕缕的明漪。在这薄霭和微漪里，听着那悠然的间歇的桨声，谁能不被引入他的美梦去呢？只愁梦太多了，这些大小船儿如何载得起呀？我们这时模模糊糊的谈着明末的秦淮河的艳迹，如《桃花扇》及《板桥杂记》里所载的。我们真神往了。我们仿佛亲见那时华灯映水，画舫凌波的光景了。于是我们的船便成了历史的重载了。我们终于恍然秦淮河的船所以雅丽过于他处，而又有奇异的吸引力的，实在是许多历史的影象使然了。

秦淮河的水是碧阴阴的；看起来厚而不腻，或者是六朝金粉所凝么？我们初上船的时候，天色还未断黑，那漾漾的柔波是这样的恬静，委婉，使我们一面有水阔天空之想，一面又憧憬着纸醉金迷之境了。等到灯火明时，阴阴的变为沉沉了：黯淡的水光，像梦一

Lying down, you can chat, you can gaze into the distance, and you can also look at the houses along the riverbanks. There are the same chairs in a big boat, but prettier in a small boat. Lanterns are hung in each boat under the awning of the front cabin. The number of the lanterns, their brightness or dimness, fineness or roughness, colour or dullness is different. No matter good or bad, there is certainly a lantern for you. The lantern is a most attractive thing. When evening lowers its curtain, lanterns are lit in all the big or small boats. The double windows mirrored with radiated lights in yellow crowns, reflect filmy mists; through the mists and clouds, in the dim and dark waves, create lingering ripples. In the thin mist and gentle ripples, listening to the sound of oars so carefree and so leisurely, who will not be lured into beautiful dreams? But I'm afraid there are too many dreams, how can these big and small boats hold them all? We were casually discussing the erotic vestiges of the late Ming Dynasty, as written in the *Peach Flower Fan* and the *Ban Bridge Prose*. Our memories were stirred and we began to long for past times as if we were seeing splendid lanterns shining upon the water, painted boats riding on the water. And our boat became a recollection of the history. We suddenly realised the reason why boats on the Qinhuai River are more elegant and attractive than other places is really because they can make many historic images clear.

The water of the Qinhuai River is green and dark. It seems thick but not oily, or is it curdled by the face powder of the beautiful women during the period of Six Dynasties? When we first got on the boat, it was not completely dark; the soft rippling waves were so peaceful, so gentle. Not only did they make us have dreams as wide as the water and the sky, they made us dream of the wonderful feeling of being in luxury and anticipation. When the lights were on, dimness turned into darkness; the dull water was

般；那偶然闪烁着的光芒，就是梦的眼睛了。我们坐在舱前，因了那隆起的顶棚，仿佛总是昂着首向前走着似的；于是飘飘然如御风而行的我们，看着那些自在的湾泊着的船，船里走马灯般的人物，便像是下界一般，迢迢的远了，又像在雾里看花，尽朦朦胧胧的。这时我们已过了利涉桥，望见东关头了。沿路听见断续的歌声：有从沿河的妓楼飘来的，有从河上船里度来的。我们明知那些歌声，只是些因袭的言词，从生涩的歌喉里机械的发出来的；但它们经了夏夜的微风的吹漾和水波的摇拂，袅娜着到我们耳边的时候，已经不单是她们的歌声，而混着微风和河水的密语了。于是我们不得不被牵惹着，震撼着，相与浮沉于这歌声里了。从东关头转湾，不久就到大中桥。大中桥共有三个桥拱，都很阔大，俨然是三座门儿；使我们觉得我们的船和船里的我们，在桥下过去时，真是太无颜色了。桥砖是深褐色，表明它的历史的长久；但都完好无缺，令人太息于古昔工程的坚美。桥上两旁都是木壁的房子，中间应该有街路？这些房子都破旧了，多年烟熏的迹，遮没了当年的美丽。我想象秦淮河的极盛时，在这样宏阔的桥上，特地盖了房子，必然是髹漆得富富丽丽的；晚间必然是灯火通明的。现在却只剩下一片黑沉沉！

like a dream, and the occasional twinkling lights were the eyes of the dream. We were sitting in the front of the cabin. Because the ceiling was bulgy, it seemed that the boat was walking proudly forward forever; as if we were floating and flying on the wind, looking at those loosely moored boats and hurrying people in the boats; as if we came from the Heaven to the earth, the journey was so far away; as if we were looking at flowers through mists, even though filmy and foggy. After we passed the Lise Bridge, the East Pass was in our view. Fitful songs could be heard during our trip: some were from brothels along the banks, and some came from boats on the river. We knew those songs had been used before, not coming through smooth throats naturally, but after being soothed by the gentle summer wind and rocked by the rippling evening waves, when they curled into our ears, they were not only songs, but mixed with intimate whispers of breeze and water. As a result, we had to be entangled, shaken, sunk and floated with the songs. No sooner had we changed our direction at the East Pass than we got to the Big Middle Bridge. It has three broad arches, like three wide proud doorways. They made us feel insignificant when we were passing under them, us on our boat too small to be noticed. The bricks of the bridge were dark brown, indicating their long history. All of them were perfectly preserved. We were amazed by the strong and beautiful ancient work. On both sides of the bridge, there were houses whose walls were made of wood. Ought there to be a road between them? These houses were old and shabby; year after year of soot and smoke had hidden their original beauty. The houses built on such a wide and big bridge allowed me to imagine how this area had looked when it had flourished. They must have been painted magnificently, and looked very bright at night with lights on. But now only vast darkness was left! Anyway, the houses built on the

但是桥上造着房子，毕竟使我们多少可以想见往日的繁华；这也慰情聊胜无了。过了大中桥，便到了灯月交辉，笙歌彻夜的秦淮河；这才是秦淮河的真面目哩。

大中桥外，顿然空阔，和桥内两岸排着密密的人家的大异了。一眼望去，疏疏的林，淡淡的月，衬着蓝蔚的天，颇像荒江野渡光景；那边呢，郁丛丛的，阴森森的，又似乎藏着无边的黑暗：令人几乎不信那是繁华的秦淮河了。但是河中眩晕着的灯光，纵横着的画舫，悠扬着的笛韵，夹着那吱吱的胡琴声，终于使我们认识绿如茵陈酒的秦淮水了。此地天裸露着的多些，故觉夜来的独迟些；从清清的水影里，我们感到的只是薄薄的夜——这正是秦淮河的夜。大中桥外，本来还有一座复成桥，是船夫口中的我们的游踪尽处，或也是秦淮河繁华的尽处了。我的脚曾踏过复成桥的脊，在十三四岁的时候。但是两次游秦淮河，却都不曾见着复成桥的面；明知总在前途的，却常觉得有些虚无缥缈似的。我想，不见倒也好。这时正是盛夏。我们下船后，借着新生的晚凉和河上的微风，暑气已渐渐销散；到了此地，豁然开朗，身子顿然轻了——习习的清风荏苒在面上，手上，衣上，这便又感到了一缕新凉了。南京的日光，大概没有杭州猛烈；西湖的夏夜老是热蓬蓬的，水像沸着一般，秦淮

bridge allowed us to picture the most flourishing period of that era, which was better than nothing. After the Big Middle Bridge, we came to the Qinhuai River where lights and moon were mixed together, and all night long filled with flutes and songs. That was the real face of the Qinhuai River.

Outside the Big Middle Bridge, it became suddenly broader, very different from the houses standing closely inside. We looked into the distance, sparse trees and a pale moon set off a blue sky, and it seemed that we were in a desolate river. Over there, the green was so deep, a bit scary, as if endless darkness was hidden. It made us doubt whether it was indeed the bustling Qinhuai River. But at length the dizzy lights in the river, the painted and crisscross boats, the melodious flutes, and the squeaky sound of Huqin made us know Qinhuai's water - green as grass, old as vintage wine. Here, the sky was bared more, so we felt the night was late. From the shadows of the clear water, we could only feel a light night - that was Qinhuai River's night. From the boatman's mouth, out of the Big Middle Bridge, it should be the Fu Cheng Bridge, which was our destination, and which should be the most flourishing place on the Qinhuai River. My feet had stepped on the back of the Fu Cheng Bridge when I was thirteen or fourteen years old. I had visited the Qinhuai River twice, but I missed the face of the Fu Cheng Bridge. I certainly knew it was just ahead, but it always seemed vague to me. So I thought it might be better not to see it. In this mid-summer, after we got off the boat, with the fresh evening coolness and the river breezes, the heat was dispersing. We reached an open place, and our bodies became light suddenly - we could feel the gentle wind on our faces, on hands, on clothes; we also felt a new wisp of coolness. Sunshine in Nianjing perhaps is not as fierce as in Hangzhou; summer evenings in the West Lake are always hot, as if its water has been

河的水却尽是这样冷冷地绿着。任你人影的憧憧，歌声的扰扰，总像隔着一层薄薄的绿纱面幂似的；它尽是这样静静的，冷冷的绿着。我们出了大中桥，走不上半里路，船夫便将船划到一旁，停了桨由它宕着。他以为那里正是繁华的极点，再过去就是荒凉了；所以让我们多多赏鉴一会儿。他自己却静静的蹲着。他是看惯这光景的了，大约只是一个无可无不可。这无可无不可，无论是升的沉的，总之，都比我们高了。

那时河里闹热极了；船大半泊着，小半在水上穿梭似的来往。停泊着的都在近市的那一边，我们的船自然也夹在其中。因为这边略略的挤，便觉得那边十分的疏了。在每一只船从那边过去时，我们能画出它的轻轻的影和曲曲的波，在我们的心上；这显着是空，且显着是静了。那时处处都是歌声和凄厉的胡琴声，圆润的喉咙，确乎是很少的。但那生涩的，尖脆的调子能使人有少年的，粗率不拘的感觉，也正可快我们的意。况且多少隔开些儿听着，因为想象与渴慕的做美，总觉更有滋味；而竞发的喧嚣，抑扬的不齐，远近的杂沓，和乐器的嘈嘈切切，合成另一意味的谐音，也使我们无所适从，如随着大风而走。这实在因为我们的心枯涩久了，变为脆弱；故偶然润泽一下，便疯狂似的不能自主了。但秦淮河确也腻人。即如船里的人面，无论是和我们一堆儿泊着的，无论是从我们眼前过去的，总是模模糊糊的，甚至渺渺茫茫的；任你张圆了眼睛，揩净

boiled, but Qinhuai's water is always so cool and green. No matter how flickered by shadows of people, troubled by songs, it always seems to wear a thin green veil. The water is so quiet, the green is so cool. Soon after we came out of the Big Middle Bridge for half a mile, the boatman rowed our boat to a place, and stopped there. He thought that was the limit of the most prosperous part of the Qinhuai River, beyond that place it would be isolated, so he let us enjoy it a bit longer there. The scene was so familiar to him he crouched silently unimpassioned by his surroundings.

It was so busy in the river at that time. More than half of the boats were moored, the rest of them were shuttling back and forth on the water. The moored boats were close to the city. Our boat was certainly one of them. Because it was a bit congested over here, we felt it was very wide over there. Whenever a boat was passing over there, we could draw its gentle shadows and rippling waves on our hearts, which seemed empty and quiet. Songs and sharp Huqin sounds could be heard everywhere at that time. However, round and sweet voices were rare. But the prickly and sharp tones could make people feel young and free, which was pleasant to us. Furthermore, filtered through our imagination and desire, the music heard from some distance sounded poignant. Also, a sudden loudness, irregular sounds both high and low, near and far, mixed with instruments' hubbub, melted into a melody with a special meaning, making us feel a sense of loss, as if blowing in the wind. This was really because for so long our hearts had been dried and withered, so when softened on this particular occasion, our longings became crazy, uncontrolled. But the Qinhuai River was hazy as well. It seemed like people's faces in boats, no matter whether moored with us or passing in front of us, they all seemed unclear, even insubstantial. It was no use opening your eyes widely and wiping off all the dirt from your eyes. There

了眦垢，也是枉然。这真够人想呢。在我们停泊的地方，灯光原是纷然的；不过这些灯光都是黄而有晕的。黄已经不能明了，再加上了晕，便更不成了。灯愈多，晕就愈甚；在繁星般的黄的交错里，秦淮河仿佛笼上了一团光雾。光芒与雾气腾腾的晕着，什么都只剩了轮廓了；所以人面的详细的曲线，便消失于我们的眼底了。但灯光究竟夺不了那边的月色；灯光是浑的，月色是清的，在浑沌的灯光里，渗入了一派清辉，却真是奇迹！那晚月儿已瘦削了两三分。她晚妆才罢，盈盈的上了柳梢头。天是蓝得可爱，仿佛一汪水似的；月儿便更出落得精神了。岸上原有三株两株的垂杨树，淡淡的影子，在水里摇曳着。它们那柔细的枝条浴着月光，就像一支支美人的臂膊，交互的缠着，挽着；又像是月儿披着的发。而月儿偶然也从它们的交叉处偷偷窥看我们，大有小姑娘怕羞的样子。岸上另有几株不知名的老树，光光的立着；在月光里照起来。却又俨然是精神矍铄的老人。远处——快到天际线了，才有一两片白云，亮得现出异彩，像美丽的贝壳一般。白云下便是黑黑的一带轮廓；是一条随意画的不规则的曲线。这一段光景，和河中的风味大异了。但灯与月竟能并存着，交融着，使月成了缠绵的月，灯射着渺渺的灵辉；这正是天之所以厚秦淮河，也正是天之所以厚我们了。

这时却遇着了难解的纠纷。秦淮河上原有一种歌妓，是以歌为

was really a lot for us to think about. Where we moored, the lights had been very bright, but they were all yellow with crowns. Being yellow neither they nor their crowns shone brightly. The more lights there were, the hazier the crowns appeared. In the twisted yellow lights like multiple stars, as if the Qinhuai River was covered by a mass of foggy light. Lights melted with the fog, everything was left only in outline, and the detailed shapes of people's faces disappeared from our eyes. But lights could never be brighter than the moon. The lights were not clear, but the moon was clear. All the unclear lights mixed with the clear moonlight, it was really a wonder! That night the moon was quite slender. She just wore her evening dress, lightly balancing on the tops of the willows. The sky was a lovely lake of blue; more charming was the moon. Two or three willow trees were on the bank; the shadows were light, swinging in the water. Their slim and gentle branches were bathing in the moonlight, like the arms of beautiful girls twisted together, held together; also like the drooping hair of the moon. The moon was peeping out occasionally from behind the crossed branches, like a shy little girl. Several trees whose names we did not know were standing on the bank naked in the moonlight, like serious and energetic old men. In the distance, near the skyline, were just one or two clouds, so bright with extraordinary colour, like beautiful shells. Under the white clouds was a black outline. It was an irregular line drawn casually. The scene here was very different from the scene in the middle of the river. But the lights and the moon twisted together, melted together, the moon looked soft and sweet, the lights were giving it a remote splendour. That was why the heaven was good to the Qinhuai River and good to us.

Then we ran into real trouble. There had been some kinds of prostitutes singing songs for a living on the Qinhuai River. In the

业的。从前都在茶舫上，唱些大曲之类。每日午后一时起；什么时候止，却忘记了。晚上照样也有一回。也在黄晕的灯光里。我从前过南京时，曾随着朋友去听过两次。因为茶舫里的人脸太多了，觉得不大适意，终于听不出所以然。前年听说歌妓被取缔了，不知怎的，颇涉想了几次——却想不出什么。这次到南京，先到茶舫上去看看，觉得颇是寂寥，令我无端的怅怅了。不料她们却仍在秦淮河里挣扎着，不料她们竟会纠缠到我们，我于是很张皇了。她们也乘着"七板子"，她们总是坐在舱前的。舱前点着石油汽灯，光亮眩人眼目：坐在下面的，自然是纤毫毕见了——引诱客人们的力量，也便在此了。舱里躲着乐工等人，映着汽灯的余辉蠕动着；他们是永远不被注意的。每船的歌妓大约都是二人；天色一黑。她们的船就在大中桥外往来不息的兜生意。无论行着的船，泊着的船，都要来兜揽的。这都是我后来推想出来的。那晚不知怎样，忽然轮着我们的船了。我们的船好好的停着，一只歌舫划向我们来的；渐渐和我们的船并着了。铄铄的灯光逼得我们皱起了眉头；我们的风尘色全给它托出来了，这使我踧踖不安了。那时一个伙计跨过船来，拿着摊开的歌折，就近塞向我的手里，说，"点几出吧"！他跨过来的时候，我们船上似乎有许多眼光跟着。同时相近的别的船上也似乎有许多眼睛炯炯的向我们船上看着。我真窘了！我也装出大方的

past, they sang songs on the tea boats. They sang from one o'clock in the afternoon till some time we did not remember. They also sang in the evening in the yellow lights with crowns. When I passed through Nanjing before, I had twice listened with my friends. Because there were too many people in the tea-boat, I felt uncomfortable and could not feel anything. I heard that singing prostitutes had been banned the year before last. I didn't know why. Several times I had wondered why they were banned, but I could not work it out. This time when I was in Nanjing, I had a look at some tea boats. They were quiet and I felt disappointed for no reason I could understand. Never realising that they were still struggling for a living on the Qinhuai River, and never realising that we would be involved, I felt very nervous. The prostitutes were also in a "Seven Paddle Boards" boat and always stayed in the front of the cabin. There, oil lights were lit, too bright to look at. Sitting there, a single strand of hair could be seen - the power of attracting guests lay in that. Men making music were hidden in the cabin. The dying light reflected the gently swaying oil lights almost imperceptibly. Normally, there were two prostitutes in one boat. When it got dark, their boats were always plying their trade around the Big Middle Bridge. No matter whether the boats were moving or moored, they would come and ask for business. I realised this afterwards. That night, I didn't know why, suddenly our boat became their object. While our boat was well moored, one singing boat was moving towards us and nearly touched our boat. Shining lights made us screw up our eyes. Our travel fatigue was displayed completely, which made me feel ill at ease. At that time, a man strode across the deck, holding a song list, and putting it into my hands, he said, "Order some songs, please." When he crossed the deck he seemed to be observed by many eyes on our boat. At the same time, it seemed as if many glaring eyes were

样子，向歌妓们瞥了一眼，但究竟是不成的！我勉强将那歌折翻了一翻，却不曾看清了几个字；便赶紧递还那伙计，一面不好意思地说，"不要，我们……不要。"他便塞给平伯。平伯掉转头去，摇手说，"不要！"那人还腻着不走。平伯又回过脸来，摇着头道，"不要！"于是那人重到我处。我窘着再拒绝了他。他这才有所不屑似的走了。我的心立刻放下，如释了重负一般。我们就开始自白了。

我说我受了道德律的压迫，拒绝了她们；心里似乎很抱歉的。这所谓抱歉，一面对于她们，一面对于我自己。她们于我们虽然没有很奢的希望；但总有些希望的。我们拒绝了她们，无论理由如何充足，却使她们的希望受了伤；这总有几分不做美了。这是我觉得很怅怅的。至于我自己，更有一种不足之感。我这时被四面的歌声诱惑了，降服了；但是远远的，远远的歌声总仿佛隔着重衣搔痒似的，越搔越搔不着痒处。我于是憧憬着贴耳的妙音了。在歌舫划来时，我的憧憬，变为盼望；我固执的盼望着，有如饥渴。虽然从浅薄的经验里，也能够推知，那贴耳的歌声，将剥去了一切的美妙；但一个平常的人像我的，谁愿凭了理性之力去丑化未来呢？我宁愿自己骗着了。不过我的社会感性是很敏锐的；我的思力能拆穿道德律的西洋镜，而我的感情却终于被它压服着，我于是有所顾忌了，

fixed on our boat from boats nearby. How embarrassed I was! But I pretended to be calm, glancing at the prostitutes, but it was no use. I managed to turn the pages of the book of songs, but I could only recognise a few words. I gave it back to the man quickly, and said in embarrassment, "We don't... we don't want any." So he gave it to Ping Bo. Ping Bo turned his head, shook his hands and said, "We don't want any." But the man still wouldn't go away. Ping Bo turned, shook his head once more and said, "We don't want that!" But the man came back to me again. I refused with embarrassment again. He went away at last with an indifferent expression. My heart at last relaxed as if a heavy burden had been thrown away. Then we began to explore our thoughts.

I think I was oppressed and influenced by morality, so I refused them, and I felt sorry in my heart. When I say "sorry", I mean on the one hand, sorry for them; and on the other, sorry for myself. Even though the prostitutes didn't expect much from us, they had at least some hopes in their hearts. We had refused them, and no matter how reasonable that was we had dashed their hopes, which was unkind. This made me feel upset. On a personal level, I felt disappointed with myself. I had been completely aroused by the songs coming from all directions, but remote songs as if scratching itches through heavy clothes, the more I scratched, the more I itched. So I longed to listen to those wonderful songs that I could hear near my ears. When the singing boat was moving towards us, my hope turned into desire. I desired so strongly, thirstily and hungrily... Even from my shallow experience, I knew that songs sung near our ears would tear all the wonder away, but would a normal person like me risk their future for some momentary sensual indulgence? I would rather deny myself. But my sense of social restraint was very sensible. My thoughts could tear morality away, but my feeling was

尤其是在众目昭彰的时候。道德律的力，本来是民众赋予的；在民众的面前，自然更显出它的威严了。我这时一面盼望，一面却感到了两重的禁制：一，在通俗的意义上，接近妓者总算一种不正当的行为；二，妓是一种不健全的职业，我们对于她们，应有哀矜勿喜之心，不应赏玩的去听她们的歌。在众目睽睽之下，这两种思想在我心里最为旺盛。她们暂时压倒了我的听歌的盼望，这便成就了我的灰色的拒绝。那时的心实在异常状态中，觉得颇是昏乱。歌舫去了，暂时宁靖之后，我的思绪又如潮涌了。两个相反的意思在我心头往复：卖歌和卖淫不同，听歌和狎妓不同，又干道德甚事？——但是，但是，她们既被逼的以歌为业，她们的歌必无艺术味的；况她们的身世，我们究竟该同情的。所以拒绝倒也是正办。但这些意思终于不曾撇开我的听歌的盼望。它力量异常坚强；它总想将别的思绪踏在脚下。从这重重的争斗里，我感到了浓厚的不足之感。这不足之感使我的心盘旋不安，起坐都不安宁了。唉！我承认我是一个自私的人！平伯呢，却与我不同。他引周启明先生的诗，"因为我有妻子，所以我爱一切的女人，因为我有子女，所以我爱一切的孩子。"

　　他的意思可以见了。他因为推及的同情，爱着那些歌妓，并且尊重着她们，所以拒绝了她们。在这种情形下，他自然以为听歌是对于她们的一种侮辱。但他也是想听歌的，虽然不和我一样，所以

oppressed by it, so I had to consider, especially when surrounded by so many onlookers. The power of morality infused by the people; in front of the people, it became more dignified. At that time, on the one hand, I was expecting to listen to the songs, on the other, I was influenced by two inhibitions: One, on the basis of popular wisdom, it's not proper behaviour to approach prostitutes; Two, prostitutes were not doing a healthy job, the attitude towards listening to their songs should not be encouraged but should be avoided. In front of all the other people's eyes, these two thoughts in my heart were so strong. They suppressed my desire to listen to the songs for the time being, and turned out to be my reluctant refusal. At that time, my heart wasn't in a normal condition. I felt a bit muddled. The singing boat went away, after short silence, my thoughts were rising like the tide again. Two contrary meanings dwelt in my heart: to sing and to prostitute someone were different, listening to songs and prostitution were different as well. Why should morality come into this matter? But, but, if they were forced to sing as a job, their songs must be tasteless. I should also have shown pity for their background. So it was right to have refused. But all these feelings didn't prevent my desire to listen to the songs. The power was so strong, and it crushed all other thoughts under its feet. In all the struggling feelings, I felt such a strong sense of dissatisfaction. This feeling made me unable to find myself at ease, not comfortable sitting or standing. Ah, I must confess that I am a selfish person. On the other hand, Ping Bo, who was not like me, quoted a poem by Mr Zhou Qimin "Because I have a wife, I love all women; because I have children, I love all children."

I knew what he meant. Because his sympathy expanded, he loved those prostitutes, respected them, and refused them. Under these circumstances, he naturally thought that it was a disgrace to

在他的心中，当然也有一番小小的争斗；争斗的结果，是同情胜了。至于道德律，在他是没有什么的；因为他很有蔑视一切的倾向，民众的力量在他是不大觉着的。这时他的心意的活动比较简单，又比较松弛，故事后还怡然自若；我却不能了。这里平伯又比我高了。

　　在我们谈话中间，又来了两只歌舫。伙计照前一样的请我们点戏，我们照前一样的拒绝了。我受了三次窘，心里的不安更甚了。清艳的夜景也为之减色。船夫大约因为要赶第二趟生意，催着我们回去；我们无可无不可的答应了。我们渐渐和那些晕黄的灯光远了，只有些月色冷清清的随着我们的归舟。我们的船竟没个伴儿，秦淮河的夜正长哩！到大中桥近处，才遇着一只来船。这是一只载妓的板船，黑漆漆的没有一点光。船头上坐着一个妓女；暗里看出，白地小花的衫子，黑的下衣。她手里拉着胡琴，口里唱着青衫的调子。她唱得响亮而圆转；当她的船箭一般驶过去时，余音还袅袅的在我们耳际，使我们倾听而向往。想不到在弩末的游踪里，还能领略到这样的清歌！这时船过大中桥了，森森的水影，如黑暗张着巨口，要将我们的船吞了下去，我们回顾那渺渺的黄光，不胜依恋之情；

listen to their songs. But he did want to listen to the songs as well. Although not like me, in his heart, there was a small conflict. The result of the conflict, sympathy won. As to morality, it wasn't important to him, because he had a tendency to disdain everything, he could hardly feel the power of other people. The sentiments in his heart were rather simple and loose, and he could feel careless afterwards. But I could not be like him. Ping Bo was better than me here.

While we were talking, another two singing boats came along. The men invited us to place an order like the former one had, and we refused them as before. I had been embarrassed three times. The uncomfortable feeling in my heart was even stronger. The delicate and charming night scene felt less agreeable because of this. The boatman, going to do his next job, urged us to return. We agreed reluctantly. Those yellow misty lights were farther and farther away from our returning boat, which was only accompanied by the cool moonlight. Long was the night of the Qinhuai River! Not until we came to the Big Bridge did we meet a boat coming from the other direction. That was a board boat carrying prostitutes, dark without a single light. A prostitute was sitting in front of the boat. We saw her in the darkness. She was wearing a white blouse with small flowers and black trousers. With her hands, she played the Huqin; with her mouth, she sang men's songs. She was singing so loudly and full-throatedly. As her boat passed by like an arrow, echoes of her song still lingered in our ears, made us long for it and lend our ears to hear it. Never had we thought that we would enjoy such a good voice at the end of our journey. At that time, our boat was passing the Big Middle Bridge. The shadow of black water like the darkness of night was opening its huge mouth, was going to swallow our boat. We turned back to look at those yellow lights in the distance, we felt

我们感到了寂寞了！这一段地方夜色甚浓，又有两头的灯火招邀着；桥外的灯火不用说了，过了桥另有东关头疏疏的灯火。我们忽然仰头看见依人的素月，不觉深悔归来之早了！走过东关头，有一两只大船湾泊着，又有几只船向我们来着。嚣嚣的一阵歌声人语，仿佛笑我们无伴的孤舟哩。东关头转湾，河上的夜色更浓了；临水的妓楼上，时时从帘缝里射出一线一线的灯光；仿佛黑暗从酣睡里眨了一眨眼。我们默然的对着，静听那汩——汩的桨声，几乎要入睡了；朦胧里却温寻着适才的繁华的余味。我那不安的心在静里愈显活跃了！这时我们都有了不足之感，而我的更其浓厚。我们却只不愿回去，于是只能由懊悔而怅惘了。船里便满载着怅惘了。直到利涉桥下，微微嘈杂的人声，才使我豁然一惊；那光景却又不同。右岸的河房里，都大开了窗户，里面亮着晃晃的电灯，电灯的光射到水上，蜿蜒曲折，闪闪不息，正如跳舞着的仙女的臂膊。我们的船已在她的臂膊里了；如睡在摇篮里一样，倦了的我们便又入梦了。那电灯下的人物，只觉像蚂蚁一般，更不去萦念。这是最后的梦；可惜是最短的梦！黑暗重复落在我们面前，我们看见傍岸的空船上一星两星的，枯燥无力又摇摇不定的灯光。我们的梦醒了，我们知道就要上岸了；我们心里充满了幻灭的情思。

（写于 1923 年 10 月）

such an unwillingness to leave. We felt lonely! The colour of the night was very dark here, invited by the waving lights far away on both sides. There was no need to mention the light away from the bridge. After we passed the bridge, there were sparsely scattered lights on the East Pass as well. Suddenly we looked up and saw the lovely plain moon, with deep regret for having come back early! After the East Pass there were one or two big ships moored, and some boats were moving towards us. From them came songs and words so loud, as if they were mocking our lonely empty boat. We changed our direction at the East Pass - the colour of the night was even darker on the river. From the brothels by the river came out a strand, a strand of light from behind the curtains now and then, as if the darkness was twinkling its eyes in its deep sleep. We were sitting silently, listening to the bubbling sound of oars, nearly asleep in dimness, searching gently for the earlier prosperous feelings. My uneasy heart was more active in silence! At that time, we all felt unsatisfied. I felt this most of all. We did not want to go back, our regrets turned into disappointment. Our boat filled with disappointment. When we arrived at the Lise Bridge, we were suddenly surprised by the noise of people's voices there, and the scene was different. The windows of the houses on the right bank were wide open, with waving electric lights inside, the lights reflected on the water, winding, twinkling, without ending, like the arms of dancing fairies. Our boat was in her arms already. As if sleeping in a cradle, we were tired and nearly went to sleep. People under the lights like ants and the lingering thought couldn't be thrown away. That was the last dream, the shortest dream unfortunately! Darkness dropped in front of us again. We saw one or two lights like stars in an empty boat by the bank, faint and waving. Our dreams woke up. We knew that we were going to go on shore soon. Our hearts filled with diminishing feelings.

- Written in October 1923